Come&See

Not just a Lent Course
– more a way of life

David Adam

kevin mayhew

First published in Great Britain in 2011 by Kevin Mayhew Ltd
Buxhall, Stowmarket, Suffolk IP14 3BW
Tel: +44 (0) 1449 737978 Fax: +44 (0) 1449 737834
E-mail: info@kevinmayhewltd.com

www.kevinmayhew.com

ISBN 978 1 84867 424 0
Catalogue No. 1501300

Cover design by Rob Mortonson
© Image used under licence from Shutterstock Inc
Edited by Claire Musters
Typeset by Richard Weaver

Printed and bound in Great Britain

Contents

The real voyage of discovery consists of not in seeking new landscapes but in having new eyes.

Marcel Proust

Introduction

When I was a curate in Hartlepool I found some lines from *The Entertainer* by John Osborne challenging and disturbing:
'Have you ever got on a railway train here, got on a train to Birmingham to West Hartlepool? Or gone from Manchester to Warrington or Widnes. And as you get out, you go down the street . . . Some kids are playing in the street and you walk up to some woman standing on her doorstep . . . What can you say to her? What real piece of information, what message can you give her? Do you say "Madam, do you know Jesus died on the cross for you?". . . And then the woman, she looks back at you, and she says, "O yes, I heard all about that."'

The above quotation is an example of how many have heard the gospel stories but not experienced the impact of the Good News in their lives. I am often aware of how little is being communicated when we talk of Jesus. Even in the Church, where we preach to people who say they believe the gospel, it is often taken for granted, as though it contained no earth-shattering news and no challenge to look at how we live. The gospel, containing life-enhancing news, is too easily accepted, filed away and left conveniently untested. We ignore the challenge for it is not acceptable to a comfortable belief that asks little and expects even less. The gospel is accepted, but not allowed to influence our daily life. It is a message that has been sanitised, trivialised and rendered impotent. The gospel is 'known' but devalued because there is no real resonance in our lives. We have learnt the facts but have not had the experience. There is a great need for us to come before the living God and to become aware of the risen Lord in our midst. This is unlikely to happen unless we are willing to make space in our busy agendas, in our daily life, for God. Can you truly say, 'I seek each day to "know him and the power of the resurrection"'?

Come and See is an invitation to spend time with Jesus, to get to know him, to talk to him, to enjoy his presence and to allow him to change your life. There is often a feeling in the gospels that Jesus is 'passing by' and is either recognised or not, is either welcomed or not. He still comes to his own and his own receive him not. But to those who receive him he gives power to become children of God (see John 1:11-12). As this is an invitation to come, it is up to you whether you do so or not. So this is not a study book in the sense that you can read through it and say 'I have done that', 'I have studied that'. It is a book to change your way of living forever for it invites you to come and abide with Jesus, to stay with him and learn of him. In this way it is not a book that seeks to talk about Jesus, though it will need to do that, but rather to point you towards him: to introduce you to the living Lord. Jesus is not confined to history or to a book, he is the living Lord. He is present and with you now and you can know him, and give your love to him. Too often Christians are found discussing the Jesus of history when there is an opportunity of talking to the living Lord now. You may like to check in your own life how often you talk to Jesus and of Jesus in the present tense.

I am always worried about people who are ready to talk about God, to talk about Jesus, but not so keen to talk to them. Discussion groups can go into some wonderful theories, Bible study groups can spend time in analysis, but it can be all ideas if we are not careful. We need to be able to communicate with and to come to the living Lord. This book is an invitation to you, 'Come and See' for yourself; spend some of each day enjoying the presence of our Lord.

Jesus, the living Lord abides with us, are we willing to abide with him? This is an eye-opening and life-changing relationship, involving the heart as well as the mind; in fact it involves our whole being. It is only in this relationship that we can know what 'faith' is. Faith is not a set of propositions or even belief; it is a living vital relationship with our

God and Saviour. To have faith is to enjoy having a vital relationship with God, to abide with him. We may believe, but we cannot say we have faith in God until we seek to walk with him and talk to him. We need to discover our God is not a God who is far off but who is at hand. These words are still true 'Draw near to God and he will draw near to you' (James 4:8).

To grow in any relationship it is necessary to stop speaking, theorising and debating and to give our undivided attention to the one who is with us. We need to stop doing and to listen. How can we see or hear clearly if our mind is full of all sorts of things? The restlessness of our minds makes us lose contact with ourselves, with each other and with our God. Stillness and rest are important to our being as well as our well-being. Our actions, our way of life, need to be guided and strengthened by our experiences in the stillness. Many of us suffer from inner-noise as badly as having a radio blaring out all the time. We need to turn off from what detracts and distracts us, from what blinds us to his presence. Learn to rejoice in him who comes to you and invites you to come to him. Know that at this moment Jesus is 'passing by'. Stop and speak to him. You may simply like to say, 'You Lord are here: your presence is with me.'

Lent is meant to be a preparation time. It is to prepare us for Easter, to help us to enter into the joy of the resurrection. Too often Lent has been used to look only at the denial of ourselves, at sin and death; Lent has been seen as a time of giving up things. In this way Lent has often become a negative time. Some Christians have never got beyond the cross and the sorrows of our world. However, Lent should point us to the reality that Jesus lives and so should be life-extending and a great adventure. Lent is a time to open our eyes and our hearts, a time to commit ourselves in love to our living Lord and Saviour and to the world around us. Again, this is an invitation to 'Come and See'.

How this course works

It is my hope that this Lent course will help you to come and see more of your Lord, to enjoy a new awareness of him. For it to work best, it would be good if everyone in the group had a copy of this book, as I would suggest each person going through the chapter before you come together each week to work on it as a group. Ideally you will look at the chosen passage every day of the week preceding the meeting: this way you will be enriched and be able to enrich the lives of others.

As far as possible for your own encounter choose a place that is restful, warm, and non-distracting. You may choose to light a candle or candles to focus your attention, perhaps burn incense or place an icon in front of you. It is good to be able to close all doors and have the room to yourself. I believe each one of us needs to have a special 'holy place' of our own. It is only when we have found one holy place that all others can become holy.

The pattern I have used in each chapter is as follows:

Rest

Begin by pausing to be in his presence. Stop whatever you are doing and be still. Make room in your life for God. Too often, we are so preoccupied that God cannot find room to enter. Clear a space each day, a space in your mind and heart as well as in your daily tasks. Begin by relaxing. Let go of all tension. Let your body have rest. Check that your hands, your feet and your neck are all relaxed. Let your breathing be natural and restful. Stop you mind from racing. Every time your mind wants to wander bring it back with a word or two. You cannot empty your mind, as it will want something in it. Say to it 'Peace' and let God's peace fill your heart and mind. Let it flow into you and about you. Say quietly, 'You Lord are here and with you I find peace.' Become aware of this reality and let it bear fruit in your life.

Sit quietly in his presence. Unlike Eastern prayer, which seeks to empty oneself, we should be ever-mindful of the presence of God, and try to focus ourselves in his presence. The stillness of our being gives God a greater opportunity of speaking to us, and communicating to us through the Scriptures.

Realise

I suggest a hymn and prayers for the start of each session. The time of silence just before these is also of great importance. We need time to come before our God who is ever with us. Awareness of this reality is of the utmost importance. It is good to decide the week before who will lead this prayer time.

Read

Before reading, it is good to ask for God's guidance. You may like to use this ancient prayer each time:

Blessed Lord, who has caused all Holy Scriptures to be written for our learning: grant that we may in such ways hear them, read, mark, learn and inwardly digest them, that by patience and comfort of thy holy Word, we may embrace and ever hold fast the blessed hope of everlasting life, which thou hast given us in our Saviour Jesus Christ.

Seek to practise what you have just prayed as you read the passage chosen for the day. Remember the reading is not so much to inform the mind as to open your eyes and to move your heart. The word of God is to touch our whole being and to allow his presence to resonate in our lives.

If you are alone it is still better to read the chosen Scripture out aloud. This reading or listening is very different from the speed reading that we apply to newspapers, books and sometimes even to the Bible. Up until the late fifteenth century when people talked of 'reading' they really meant 'listening', as few people could read and those that did read,

read out aloud. For many centuries the silent scanning of a page was unknown, all reading was spoken out – even if quietly. Reading involved not just the eyes and the mind, but the mouth, tongue and the ears. It was concerned with sounds and rhythms and it was given great attention as it was received with silence, patience and receptivity. Often texts and important passages were read again and again. In all reading there was a desire to involve the heart as well as the ear. Each one of us needs to learn this ancient method of hearing with the 'ear of the heart'. This is reverential listening; listening in a spirit of silence and of awe. It is attentive; waiting upon each word as the word of God in love. Listen for the still, small voice of God that will speak to you personally – not loudly, but intimately. So read slowly, attentively, gently listening to hear a word or phrase that is God's word for you this day. Repeat important words and ideas and let them reverberate in your whole being. Concentrate on the words. Let them get deep into your attention; do not let other thoughts or events crowd them out. Allow space for God to speak to you through the written words.

After the reading I have provided what I hope is helpful background information to aid your exploration of the text. The comments are to be read before the session together as a group and not within it. They will be useful for every group member to read, but whoever is the leader for the week should make themselves familiar with the reading and the comments.

The passage of Scripture has been printed in full for each week within this book. However it is good to use a Bible and become familiar with where various books are in relationship to each other. If possible take your Bible to your study group and find the reading in your Bible. In the group I would suggest that someone other than the leader does the readings, the more that can be shared around the better. It is better if the passage is read twice, once by a female voice and once by a male voice.

Ruminate

Many of the early saints suggested we chew over the words in Scripture and that we 'inwardly digest them'. Too often the words are bolted down so that we can get on with the next course; whatever that is. Chew over the words and extract the goodness from them.

As you chew over the story or words, be aware that they are a way of God feeding you, of God reaching out to you, of God speaking to you. Ask, what does God require of you? What does he seek to do for you?

Now picture the scene. Visualise what you have just read. What images does it create? Bring each of your senses into play. Are there things you can see, touch, hear and smell? Can you see yourself within what has been read, if not, why not? Remember you are ruminating, so take your time. Imagining the event is very important, as it is the only way it can truly touch you. Ask yourself what voices are being heard and who is reacting. If you had been there, would you have liked to say anything?

If your mind wants to wander recite the key words you have picked out. Heed the guidance of St Paul in Philippians 4:4, 8, 'Rejoice in the Lord always; again I will say Rejoice ... whatever is true, whatever is honourable, whatever is just, whatever is pure, whatever is pleasing, whatever is commendable, if there is any excellence and if there is anything worthy of praise, think about these things.'

When you are working through this as a group you could talk as if you were making a film. What would need to be included to make sense of this event; how would you like it to be seen and portrayed? Pick out key words and actions from within the story. Try to build up a full picture of the event together, including the emotions of the people involved. Building up such images is important, as it helps us to become more sensitive and aware of the situation and of what is taking place.

React

Start by reacting to what you have just experienced. React towards God in prayer and thanksgiving. React towards your neighbour, the world, yourself. What action is called for out of what you have received? Jesus spoke in parables not for us to study them but for us to have an immediate reaction to them. Prayer necessitates action too. Not only do we say, 'Your will be done' we have to seek out God's will and then do it.

When working through this section with a group there are two stages to it: a silent part to speak and listen to God individually and then a part in which to communicate with each other. Both these sections demand your undivided attention. Group work is of great importance and reveals heart attitudes; those who do not really listen carefully to others are unlikely to give God their undivided attention.

During the silent part think over the relevance of the events. These were ordinary people often taking part in extraordinary events. Why do these people have a place in the Bible? What message do they have for us? What is God seeking to tell us through them? Perhaps when we seek God's meaning we should remember the statement of Julian of Norwich who said that 'love is his meaning' at all times.

Moving on to the time of communication, make sure that each person is given the opportunity to say how he or she reacts to the story. The most important part of this section is to listen to each other. God often chooses to speak to us through others. Remember, if we are not good at listening to others, it is not likely that we will be good at listening to him. We learn to give our attention to God by the way we give it to each other.

Rest and rejoice

After the hard work and concentration of each session make sure you have some time to enjoy what you have experienced and to enjoy being with each other. Be aware of where you are and whom you are with. Appreciate your surroundings and the generosity of your host. You should make sure you get to know all the members of your group better. It is good to be able to thank people for their insight and sharing. We ought to be able to show we are genuinely interested in the people we spend time with.

Again this last section has two parts. First, turn to the ever-present God and rejoice in him. Like earthly lovers often find, there is no need for words: rest in him, in his power, his peace and his love. This part can be compared to sunbathing; lie back in the presence and just enjoy being there. Wallow in the reality that you are in the heart of God and that God is in your heart. Quietly rejoice in the fact that 'We abide in him and he in us' (1 John 4:13).

After the time of quiet it is good to end the session with music and prayer. For this reason I have suggested hymns and prayers. Do remember that these suggestions are guides and feel free to select and use your own choices. I have purposely ended each session with a blessing. Blessings express the reality of the love of God towards us; they are not requests for a blessing as much as an acknowledgement that God does bless us. He offers us the greatest blessing, which is his loving presence.

The session is now finished, but try to come away from it gently rather than abruptly.

Recollect

This part should be used during the days following a session. Let the seeds that were sown grow in you: seek to reap the harvest and be fed by the word. The whole point of the recollection is to affirm that you are in the presence of God and held in his love. If you can, have a short prayer or a sentence you are able to use during the days ahead that could help to let your new awareness sink home. Recollect once or twice each day. I have suggested short prayers and texts that might be of help but it is important that you choose something you can make your own so either personalise my suggestions or choose something yourself.

The six parts, or 'movements', of the session may not always follow a linear progression. Allow yourself or the group some freedom. The aim is to move into the depths of silence and stillness where we can hear the word spoken to us in love and respond.

As you are coming to see and abide with a loved one, the joy and the excitement of that coming needs to be captured. As with any visit with a friend, you need to prepare; you may have to alter your daily schedule, even clean out a room. The important thing is to be as ready as possible for them and to enjoy being with them. As most of us these days are busy people, that means pencilling space into your diary, making sure your day is not overloaded. It is no different in our dealings with God. For many it is not that they do not believe, it is that they do not give God space or time. Be aware of the one who is 'passing by' and enjoy knowing that you are invited to 'Come and See'.

Tips for group leaders

For you to be an effective leader it is best for you to have worked through the session at home, preferably two or three times before your group session. It is important to plan out the meeting so I have given a rough idea of how long each section should be opposite. Though you will need to be a good timekeeper to ensure the session doesn't run over, you should also have the freedom to decide if a particular section wants to be shortened or lengthened. Whatever amendments you may make, it is important to begin and end on time. The whole session should last for just over an hour.

Rest *(5 minutes)*

Realise *(10 minutes)*

Read *(10 minutes)*

Ruminate *(in silence 5 minutes, shared 5 minutes)*

React *(directed to God 5 minutes, shared with the group 10 minutes)*

Rest and rejoice *(in silence for 2 minutes, final prayers, music and blessing 5–8 minutes)*

Try and keep the whole session within an agreed time schedule. There is nothing worse than feeling trapped in meetings that last too long. However, if people decide to linger after a meeting that is another matter and you can enjoy further time together if agreed.

Lent 1

John the Baptist: Behold, the Lamb of God

Rest (*5 minutes*)

We come to so much of life distracted. We may be living in the present but so much of the time are looking ahead to what is coming. We have got used to racing ahead. We all need to learn to be still, to make space in our lives for the now and for the presence of God. We should heed the words of Jesus, 'Come to me, all you that are weary and are carrying heavy burdens, and I will give you rest' (Matthew 11:28).

At the beginning of your approach to God it is important that you let go of the need for haste, let go of all agendas and all tension and learn to rest in his presence. Still your body and let it relax, bit by bit. Start with you face and neck, then your shoulders and check over your whole body for signs of tension. Seek to be still and comfortable, open to the God who comes to you. Clear your mind of clutter and wandering thoughts, then gently concentrate it on God, on his love and his presence with you. If it begins to wander, say, 'You Lord are here: your Spirit is with me.'

Realise (*10 minutes*)

Start by saying the following affirmation together:

We are in the presence, the peace and the power of God the Father, the Son and the Holy Spirit. Amen

Hymn

Be still and know that I am God

Choose someone to lead you in the following prayers:

'Among you stands one whom you do not know' (John 1:26).
The Lord is here.
His Spirit is with us.

'He was in the world, and the world came into being through him; yet the world did not know him' (John 1:10).
The Lord is here.
His Spirit is with us.

'He came to what was his own, and his own people did not accept him' (John 1:11).
The Lord is here.
His Spirit is with us.

'But to all who received him, who believed in his name, he gave power to become children of God' (John 1:12).
The Lord is here
His Spirit is with us.

Blessed are you Lord God of all creation, to you be praise and glory forever. You send to us men and women of vision to declare your love and to reveal your presence with us. Your messenger John the Baptist, pointed the way to Jesus and told us he is the Lamb of God who will take away the sin of the world. May we learn to share in the witness to Christ and point others towards him and his saving power that we all may rejoice in him and in his love.
Blessed are you, our God for ever and ever.

Lord, inspire us by the word and witness of John the Baptist to turn to you each day,
to see you as our Lord and Saviour,
to know you as the Lamb of God who takes away
the sin of the world,
and to abide in your presence and in your peace
now and always.

Eternal God, the light of the minds that know you,
the joy of the hearts that love you,
the strength of the wills that serve you;
grant us so to know you that we may truly love you,
so to love you that we may freely serve you, to the glory of
your holy name. **Amen**

Gelasian Sacramentary, 5th century

Read *(10 minutes)*

John 1:19-34

[19]This is the testimony given by John when the Jews sent priests and Levites from Jerusalem to ask him, 'Who are you?' [20]He confessed and did not deny it, but confessed, 'I am not the Messiah.' [21]And they asked him, 'What then? Are you Elijah?' He said, 'I am not.' 'Are you the prophet?' He answered, 'No.' [22]Then they said to him, 'Who are you? Let us have an answer for those who sent us. What do you say about yourself?' [23]He said, 'I am the voice of one crying out in the wilderness, "Make straight the way of the Lord,"' as the prophet Isaiah said.

[24]Now they had been sent from the Pharisees. [25]They asked him, 'Why then are you baptising if you are neither the Messiah, nor Elijah, nor the prophet?' [26]John answered them, 'I baptise with water. Among you stands one whom you do not know, [27]the one who is coming after me; I am not worthy to untie the thong of his sandal.' [28]This took place in Bethany across the Jordan where John was baptising.

[29]The next day he saw Jesus coming toward him and declared, 'Here is the Lamb of God who takes away the sin of the world! [30]This is he of whom I said, "After me comes a man who ranks ahead of me because he was before me." [31]I myself did not know him; but I came baptising with water for this reason, that he might be revealed to Israel.' [32]And John testified, 'I saw the Spirit descending from heaven like a dove, and it remained on him. [33]I myself did not know him, but the one who sent me to baptise with water said to me, "He on whom you see the Spirit descend and remain is the one who baptises with the Holy Spirit." [34]And I myself have seen and have testified that this is the Son of God.'

Comments

John is visited by officials from Jerusalem. St John's Gospel describes these visitors as '*Ioudaioi*', which is translated 'Jews' and this word is used in this Gospel 70 times. But we must remember that Jesus is a Jew and John the Baptist is a Jew. The word John uses here is for the Jews that oppose Jesus. John is visited by priests and Levites because he is a Levite – as was his father Zechariah (Luke 1:5). It would seem to the Levites that John did not conform to what was their perception of how a Levite should behave. The Pharisees also wanted to check John's credentials to make sure he was not a false prophet. As is the case throughout history, the established Church is fearful of change and anything new.

They confront John the Baptist wanting to know if he thinks he is the Messiah. If he did think he was, he would face an inquisition! John denies this claim but the wording in Greek stresses the word *I* by its position. It is as if John is saying 'I am not the Messiah, but if you only knew he is here.'

They go on to ask, if not the Messiah 'are you Elijah'. There was a belief that Elijah would come again to prepare the world for the coming of the Messiah (Malachi 4:5). John says, 'No' once more. Again they ask if he is the prophet that is expected to come to prepare the way for the Messiah. He says 'No' to this. He does not see himself fulfilling such high traditional expectations. They need to take a message back to those who sent them, so they persist and ask John, 'Who are you then? What do you say for yourself? In the words of Isaiah (40:3) John describes himself as a 'voice' calling people to be ready for the coming of the Lord. Now they ask, 'But why are you baptising?' John's answer is a challenge rather than a reply. He tells them there is one standing among them whom they do not recognise. John's whole aim is to point people towards the Lord. He believes they should not spend their time looking at him but look to the coming one; the coming king.

The next day John sees Jesus coming towards him and proclaims, 'Here is the Lamb of God who takes way the sin of the world.' He also declares that the reason for his baptism was to prepare for the revealing of Jesus to Israel. John tells of the Spirit of God descending on Jesus like a dove, and the Voice that said to him that the one on whom he sees the Spirit descend is the one who baptises with the Holy Spirit. John now declares of Jesus, 'This is the Son of God.'

In John's Gospel, John the Baptist's whole aim is to point to Jesus, to prepare the way for Jesus to enter into people's lives. He does not seek to draw people to himself except to then send them to Jesus. In John's Gospel there is no reference to John calling for repentance or forgiveness for this is the part work of Jesus: it is Jesus who takes away the sin of the world.

Ruminate *(in silence 5 minutes, shared 5 minutes)*

Start in silence, each one picturing the scene in your minds. Be aware of the conflict with the authorities. Seek to feel the reaction of John and his disciples.

What did John mean when he called Jesus 'the Lamb of God' and the 'Son of God'? Do you have a favourite title for Jesus?

As a group

Imagine you are on a film set. Seek to show the honest probing of the priests and Levites but also how they were restricted by their own prejudices. Show John's desire to point them towards Jesus.

React *(directed to God, 5 minutes, shared with the group, 10 minutes)*

Give thanks to God for the sending of his Son into the world and turn to Jesus in prayer. Use the descriptions of Jesus on the next page.

John describes Jesus as 'Lord' (v23). Have you accepted him as your Lord? Do you see him and know him as the 'King of kings and Lord of lords?' How do you show this in your life? *Pray:* 'Jesus my Lord I you adore. Make me love you more and more.'

'Among you stands one whom you do not know' (v26). How true this is. Jesus can be with us, in our midst and we fail to recognise him. Too often he is ignored or we find no room for him. You need to spend time in his presence if you are to get to know him. Jesus of Nazareth is passing by. Invite him to spend some time with you now, talk to him, rest in his love and his presence.
Pray: 'Come to my heart Lord Jesus, there is room in my heart for you.'

'The Lamb of God, who takes away the sin of the world' (v29). As a Levite John was familiar with the daily ritual at the Temple: every morning and every evening a lamb was sacrificed in the Temple for the sin of the people (Exodus 29:38-39). John was suggesting it is not lambs that take away our sin but only the offering of Jesus. The other image this reminds us of is the Passover lamb. The blood of the Passover lamb is a sign of how the children of Israel were saved from death and rescued from a life of captivity. They were freed to set off for the Promised Land. Jesus will bring you into his glorious freedom if you will let him. He will rescue you from death and give you, even now, life which is eternal.
Pray: 'Jesus, deliver us from all evil and keep us in life eternal.'

John declares he did not know the Messiah, but his actions were to prepare the way for him to be revealed to Israel. John sees himself as a pointer to the Christ (v31).
Pray: 'Lord that I might know you and your love.'

Jesus is the one 'on whom . . . the Spirit descend(s)' (v33). Though there is no specific reference to the baptism of Jesus in this Gospel, John is revealing what he experienced at the baptism of Jesus. Jesus is the 'anointed one', as he is anointed by the Spirit of God. Jesus is the one who 'baptises with the Holy Spirit' (v33). Do we live as people immersed in the Spirit?

Pray: 'Lord may I know that I dwell in you and that you are in me.'

As a group

Choose the words of John the Baptist from this passage that speak to you the most and share your thoughts on them with the group. Make sure you give everyone a chance to say which of the sayings speak most to them.

End by saying together:
You, Lord, are here and with us now.

Rest and rejoice (*silence for 2 minutes, final prayers, music and blessing 5–8 minutes*)

Know that Jesus comes to you in the silence. Rest and rejoice in his presence. Enjoy spending this time with him. Offer your love to him afresh. Acknowledge that he is with you and say to him, 'My Saviour and my God.' Know that as he comes to you he wants you to come to him.

Final prayers and music

Read this prayer quietly to yourselves, and then say it altogether:

Come, true light
Come life eternal . . .
Come for your name fills our hearts with longing
and is ever on our lips;
yet who you are and what your nature is,
we cannot say or know.

Come, Alone to the alone.
Come for you are yourself the desire that is within me.
Come for you are the consolation of my humble soul.
Come for you are, my joy, my endless delight.

Symeon the New Theologian (949–1022)

Let someone pray this prayer, announce the hymn and give
the blessing:

Lord Jesus, there are times when I do not notice
your coming to me:
times when I have ignored your presence.
There are times when my senses are dull:
when my mind begins to doubt you.
Lord, lead me out of my darkness into your light.
Lord, lead me from my loneliness to the joy of your presence,
until I come out of the wilderness, and emptiness
and share the joys of the Promised Land.

Hymn

Choose one of the following to sing together:

On Jordan's bank the Baptist's cry
Just as I am without one plea
Hark a thrilling voice is calling

The blessing

God,
who called John the Baptist to prepare the way for his Son,
open your eyes to the coming of our Lord,
open your heart to his love,
that you may be aware that he is with you.
And the blessing of God Almighty,
the Father, the Son and the Holy Spirit,
be upon you and remain with you always. **Amen**

Recollect

Take away with you a thought, a text or a resolution to use during the week. Always include in this a reminder of God's presence and use it every day as often as possible.

Suggestion: Think upon 'Among you stands a one whom you do not know' (v26) and pray: 'Lord that I may know you and in knowing you love you.'

Lent 2

Jesus: Come and see

Rest (*5 minutes*)

Just as a car cannot keep running without refuelling we cannot keep pouring ourselves out without being refilled and renewed. Many people are going about totally drained because they have not allowed themselves the time to be renewed. Stop all activity and allow God the time and space to refresh you and renew you. Make sure you are relaxed in body and mind. Hear our Lord say, 'Come to me . . . and I will give you rest' (Matthew 11:28). Let the love of God enfold you. If you feel your mind wandering you may like to say:

God to enfold me,
God to surround me,
God in my speaking,
God in my thinking.

God in my sleeping,
God in my waking,
God in my watching,
God in my hoping.

God in my life,
God in my lips,
God in my soul,
God in my heart.

Alexander Carmichael, The Carmina Gadelica, Volume 3

Realise (*10 minutes*)

Start by saying the following prayer together:

We are in the presence, the peace and the power of God, the Father, the Son and the Holy Spirit. Amen

Hymn
Reach out and touch the Lord

Get someone to read out the following:
'The Word became flesh and lived among us' (John 1:14).
The Lord is here.
His Spirit is with us.

'And we have seen his glory, the glory as of a father's only son, full of grace and truth' (John 1:14).
The Lord is here.
His Spirit is with us.

'Jesus of Nazareth is passing by' (Luke 18:37).
The Lord is here.
His Spirit is with us.

'Look, here is the Lamb of God' (John 1:36).
The Lord is here.
His Spirit is with us.

Blessed are you, Lord God of all creation,
to you be praise and glory for ever!
In the wilderness of this world you have sent us
prophets and preachers to show us the way into
your presence and love.
As we rejoice in the ministry of John the Baptist
let us look beyond him to you and your glory:
let us rejoice that your presence is near to each of us
and come to you in this time of stillness.
Blessed are you, Father, Son and Holy Spirit.

God of all grace and goodness,
grant us a mind to perceive you
and a heart ready to welcome you,
that your Son Jesus Christ, in his coming,
may find us ready to follow to him
and dwell with him.

May he find in us a dwelling prepared for him:
who is alive and reigns with you and the Holy Spirit,
one God now and for ever.

Read *(10 minutes)*

John 1:35-9

> [35]The next day John again was standing with two of his disciples, [36]and as he watched Jesus walk by, he exclaimed, 'Look, here is the Lamb of God!'
> [37]The two disciples heard him say this, and they followed Jesus. [38]When Jesus turned and saw them following, he said to them, 'What are you looking for?' They said to him, 'Rabbi' (which translated means Teacher), 'where are you staying?' [39]He said to them, 'Come and see.' They came and saw where he was staying, and they remained with him that day. It was about four o'clock in the afternoon.

Comments

Jesus is present again and is 'passing by'. Here is a great opportunity, as there always is in the presence of Jesus. John is with two of his own disciples but he points them away from himself and to Jesus. 'Look,' he says, 'here is the Lamb of God.' He knows in doing this he is sending his disciples away from himself and to Jesus. John does not aim to attach people to himself but wants them to come to Jesus. The disciples follow Jesus. It would seem that they kept their distance from him, following in his steps but not close to him. Jesus did what was typical of him; he turns and speaks to them. This is the action of God so often if we turn towards him we find he comes to meet us. 'Draw near to God and he will draw near to you' (James 4:8). He never forces himself upon us but always give us the choice; it is up to us whether we make contact or not (see John 1:11-13). We could not even have begun to seek God until he had first come to us. It was him who put the desire to know him in our hearts.

Jesus asks them, 'What are you looking for?' This is a question we need to ask ourselves every now and again. What are we seeking from life? What are our priorities? The disciples answer 'Rabbi, where are you staying?' They are not just asking him where he resides but are saying they want to go with him. They did not want him as a passing acquaintance on the road: they wanted to abide with him. They wanted to spend time with him, give attention to him and to learn from him.

Jesus invites them to 'Come and see.' The Jewish Rabbis used this phrase when they were leading their followers into deeper realms. It was used to invite students to share and discover with their teacher the areas of his expertise. Jesus was inviting the disciple to come and discover in him what only he could reveal to them. They remained with him that day.

'It was about four o' clock in the afternoon.' This was a momentous moment when life was changed forever. It was a time that would never be forgotten.

Ruminate *(in silence 5 minutes, shared 5 minutes)*

Start in silence and consider that Jesus is 'passing by': there is a sense in which this is always true. Jesus invited these disciples to 'Come and see'. Now realise that he is inviting you too. Come to him in the quiet. Invite him into your home and your life. You may like to use these words of a hymn as a prayer:

'Be near me Lord Jesus, I ask thee to stay close by for ever and love me I pray.'

In the stillness pray:

'Lord open my eyes to you presence: open my heart to your love. Let me know you are with me now and always.'

As a group

In this passage John points away from himself. This is the work of every preacher and every priest – to direct the attention away from himself and towards God. It is the priest's task to open our eyes to the mystery of the presence in our midst: teaching us to look with the eyes of the heart. Discuss how the Church seeks to point people to Jesus, in its liturgy, ministry and in the layout of a church. Does the Church sometimes promote itself when it should be drawing people to God? How can we improve the way we bring people before our God?

React *(directed to God 5 minutes, shared with the group 10 minutes)*

In the stillness be aware that Jesus is always 'passing by'. You are often unaware of him. He is waiting for you to recognise him or not. Seek to discover that he calls you at all stages of your life, in joys and in sorrows, in times of doubt and fear as well as in times of awareness and worship. He invites you to follow in his way. He invites you to 'Come and see', to stay with him and experience his love and presence for yourself.

As a group

Share what struck you most about this passage. Then each one describe when you turned to Jesus and found his presence, or when he found you.

Let different people lead you in the following prayers:

'The Lamb of God.'

Pray together:

**Lamb of God,
deliver from captivity of sin and death.**

**Bring us out of darkness into your light
into the freedom of the Promised Land
where we may rejoice in your presence and saving power.**

John the Baptist said, 'He must increase, but I must decrease.'

Pray together:

**Lord Jesus to you I pray
that I may grow more like you
day by day.**

'They follow Jesus.'

Pray together:

**Lord Jesus I seek to follow in your steps.
When I stray guide me back to you.
When I get lost turn to me in love
and draw me to yourself.**

What are you looking for?

Pray together:

**Lord Jesus,
help me to keep a clear vision
of what truly matters in life
and how to walk in your ways.**

Rest and rejoice *(in silence for 2 minutes, final prayer, music and blessing 5–8 minutes)*

Silently give thanks for the coming of Jesus Christ into the world and for his presence with you.

Spend this time talking to him individually.

Final prayers and music

Say together these two prayers:

Thanks be to you,
my Lord Jesus Christ,
for all the benefits you have won for me,
for all the pain and insults you have borne for me.
O merciful Redeemer, Friend and Brother,
may I know you more clearly,
love you more dearly,
and follow you more nearly,
day by day.

St Richard of Chichester (1197–1253)

Lord, come make your home with me:
in the stillness speak to me
in your love turn to me,
to my restlessness come with your peace.
Lord, draw me to yourself
and then send me out to tell of you.
I ask this in your name, Jesus Christ my Lord.

*Let the leader announce the hymn and afterwards say the
blessing prayer.*

Hymn

Pick one from the following list to sing together:

Jesus calls us; o'er the tumult
Just as I am
O Jesus I have promised

The blessing

May the Christ who comes, be known to dwell with you:
may the peace of his presence enfold you:
may the power of his love be known to you:
and the blessing of God Almighty,
the Father, the Son and the Holy Spirit
be upon you and abide with you always.

Recollect

Take away with you a thought, a text or a resolution to use during the week. Always include in this a reminder of the presence and use it every day as often as possible.

Remind yourself often this week that 'Jesus is passing by'. Invite him into your life. Know that as you turn to him he is ready to hear you and be with you.

You may like to learn or at least say the prayer of St Richard of Chichester this week.

Lent 3

Andrew: Come and see

Rest *(5 minutes)*

Every so often it is necessary to stop, to look and to listen. We need to cease from all activity, especially in an age when hyper-activity and multi-tasking is looked upon as a sign of life. The world and life does not cease if we stop doing. But we can cease to live to our full extend by being lost in busyness. Make sure your body is relaxed; check it over from head to feet, relaxing each part in turn. Give your attention to a single item. You may choose something of beauty, a candle, an icon, or you might like to visualise a peaceful scene. Rest there and know that you are in the presence of God. God has been waiting for you in love to turn to him. Hear him calling your name. Know that he loves you and gives himself to you. Rejoice in his being with you and in his peace. You do not have to do anything for God to come, for he is with you. Be open to him.

Realise *(10 minutes)*

Start by saying the following affirmation and singing the hymn together:

We are in the presence, the peace, the power of God, the Father, the Son and the Holy Spirit. Amen

Hymn

Will you come and follow me

Choose someone to lead you in the following:

'Draw near to God and he will draw near to you' (James 4:8). The Lord is here.
His Spirit is with us.

'In him we live and move and have our being.' (Acts 17:28).
The Lord is here.
His Spirit is with us.

'I have called you by name, you are mine.' (Isaiah 43:1).
The Lord is here.
His Spirit is with us.

'I heard the voice of the Lord saying,
"Whom shall I send, and who will go for us?"
And I said, "Here am I; send me"' (Isaiah 6:8).
The Lord is here.
His Spirit is with us.

Jesus said, 'Abide in me as I abide in you' (John 15:4).
The Lord is here.
His Spirit is with us.

O gracious and holy Father,
give us wisdom to perceive you,
intelligence to understand you,
diligence to seek you,
patience to wait for you,
eyes to behold you,
a heart to meditate upon you,
and a life to proclaim you,
through the power of the Spirit
of our Lord Jesus Christ.

St Benedict (480–547)

Say together:

Word of God, you call us.
Lord of life, you dwell with us.
Lord of peace, you guide us.
Lord of love, you inspire us.
Lord of grace, you empower us.

**Lord of power, send us,
that we may tell of you
and your salvation.**

Read *(10 minutes)*

John 1:40-51

[40]One of the two who heard John speak and followed him was Andrew, Simon Peter's brother. [41]He first found his brother Simon and said to him, 'We have found the Messiah' (which is translated Anointed). [42]He brought Simon to Jesus, who looked at him and said, 'You are Simon son of John. You are to be called Cephas' (which is translated Peter).

[43]The next day Jesus decided to go to Galilee. He found Philip and said to him, 'Follow me.' [44]Now Philip was from Bethsaida, the city of Andrew and Peter. [45]Philip found Nathanael and said to him, 'We have found him about whom Moses in the law and also the prophets wrote, Jesus son of Joseph from Nazareth.' [46]Nathanael said to him, 'Can anything good come out of Nazareth?' Philip said to him, 'Come and see.' [47]When Jesus saw Nathanael coming toward him, he said of him, 'Here is truly an Israelite in whom there is no deceit!' [48]Nathanael asked him, 'Where did you come to know me?' Jesus answered, 'I saw you under the fig tree before Philip called you.' [49]Nathanael replied, 'Rabbi, you are the Son of God! You are the King of Israel!' [50]Jesus answered, 'Do you believe because I told you that I saw you under the fig tree? You will see greater things than these.' [51]And he said to him, 'Very truly, I tell you, you will see heaven opened and the angels of God ascending and descending upon the Son of Man.'

Comments

This translation says of Andrew 'he first found his brother Simon'. 'First' is from the Greek word *'proton'*. Some manuscripts use the Greek word *'proi'* which means 'early in the morning'. Both reveal an urgency to communicate. Andrew tells Simon, 'We have found the Messiah.' For the non-Jewish readers the Gospel writer translates Messiah as 'Anointed' or as 'Christ'. This is a tremendous claim that Andrew can only have an inkling of but if they come to Jesus and abide with him the meaning will be revealed more and more. Do you abide with Christ and tell of him? Andrew wanted to share fully: he brought Simon to Jesus. In John's Gospel, Andrew brings various people to Jesus: Simon his brother, then a boy with five loaves and two small fish (John 6:8-9) and then, towards the end of the ministry of Jesus, the Greeks (John 12:22).

Jesus looked at Simon and said: 'You are Simon son of John. You are to be called Cephas' (which is translated Peter). Jesus accepts people as they are but he is also aware of their potential: 'you are' and 'you will' shows promise and the ability to change. In the Old Testament a new relationship with God was sometimes shown by the person being given a new name. When God made a covenant with Abram, he said to him, 'your name shall be Abraham' (Genesis 17:5). In the same way when Jacob wrestled with God at the ford of Jabbok, he was told, 'you shall no longer be called Jacob but Israel' (Genesis 32:28). In naming Simon 'Peter', which means 'rock', Jesus signified the potential within this fisherman. In Jesus we can do great things that we cannot do alone.

The scene changes and we are in another day and in another part of the country. Jesus has moved north to Galilee and there found Philip. Until now Jesus has been pointed out by John the Baptist, followed by Andrew and another disciple. Andrew claims to have found Jesus and then found his brother Simon and brings him to Jesus. Each has come to Jesus through someone else's direction. Yet sometimes there is a direct encounter: Jesus found Philip and said to him, 'Follow me' (v43). No doubt we would like to have known more about this. All we are told is that he came from Bethsaida, the fishing town that was the home to Andrew and Peter. The important thing to note is that Philip responded to the call. Philip found Nathanael and said to him, 'We have found him about whom Moses in the law and also the prophets wrote, Jesus son of Joseph from Nazareth' (v45). While there are great claims for Jesus in his fulfilling the Law and the Prophets, Nathanael seizes on the earthly side and asks if anything good can come out of Nazareth. The Scriptures had not singled Nazareth out for any honours and Nathanael did not think highly of it. It would have been easy to have become involved in debate but Philip simply invites him, 'Come and see' (v46).

Jesus again looks and sees potential, describing Nathanael as an Israelite in whom there is no guile. Nathanael, no doubt flattered and yet surprised at such a comment, asks, 'Where did you come to know me?' (v48). Jesus told him how he saw him under the fig tree and for reasons unknown to us this fills Nathanael with wonder and awe. He replies to Jesus, 'Rabbi, you are the Son of God! You are the King of Israel!' (v49). Nathanael had been captured by Jesus. Here is an amazing confession of faith. Jesus is not only a teacher, he is the Son of God and the Anointed One of Israel.

Ruminate *(in silence 5 minutes, shared 5 minutes)*

Picture the scene between Andrew and his brother Simon. Visualise the excitement and joy of Andrew and the wonder, if not puzzlement, of Simon.

Then picture Andrew bringing his brother to Jesus and Simon's encounter with him. How must Simon have felt? What would he have made of his new name?

As a group

Those who come to Jesus cannot keep the Good News to themselves. Andrew tells Peter, Philip tells Nathaniel. The Good News is for sharing. How do you personally share it?

Tell of who brought you to know the Christ and what a difference he makes to your life.

Do you allow Christ to change you and to 'send' you?

Discuss the fact that few people are won to Christ by debate. More are brought to him by simply witnessing his presence and love.

React *(directed to God 5 minutes, shared with the group 10 minutes)*

Start by individually giving thanks to 'God, whose love is all around us, who in Jesus sought and found us' (from a Fred Kaan hymn).

Give thanks for those who have shared their faith with you, for those who brought you to Jesus.

Turn to Jesus as the Son of God, your Saviour and your King and give thanks for your calling.

Know that those whom he calls he sends. Annie Dillard in *The Writing Life* says: 'The impulse to keep to yourself what you have learned is not only shameful, it is destructive. Anything you do not give freely and abundantly becomes lost to you. You open your safe and find ashes.' This is true of our faith; it needs sharing for it to grow.

Before opening up a conversation, as yourself when did you last tell anyone of Jesus, last bring someone to Jesus? This is one of the great weaknesses of modern established churches. There is a danger that Jesus is hidden behind our traditions, our liturgy and our music. We are not asked to bring people to church but to the living Lord.

As a group

Allow each one time to share what struck them most about this passage.

Discuss together how the church community can bring people to Jesus. Remember you cannot introduce people to someone you do not know.

Gustave Doré was a popular French illustrator and artist of the mid-nineteenth century, and his work included engravings for the English Bible. Once a young artist approached him and asked his opinion on a painting he had done of Jesus. Doré took a while to reply. When he did it was one sentence: 'You do not love him, or you would paint him better.' How true is this in our proclaiming of the Gospel?

Rest and rejoice *(in silence 2 minutes, final prayers, music and blessing 5–8 minutes)*
In the quietness do the following individually.

Give thanks for the Gospels and the calling of the disciples.
Pray for the outreach and mission of Christ to which he calls the Church.
Pray that you may truly know him and the power of his resurrection.

The final prayers and music
Choose someone to lead you through this section.

Set our hearts on fire with love of you, Christ our God, that in that flame we may love you with all our heart, with all our mind, with all our soul, and with all our strength and our neighbours as ourselves; so that keeping your command-ments, we may glorify you, the giver of all good gifts.

Eastern Orthodox prayer

Say this prayer together:

O Lord,
open my eyes to your passing by,
open my mind to your wonders,
open my lips to proclaim your salvation,
open my heart to your love.
Open my whole being to your healing
and let me abide with you today and for ever.
Lord, teach me to seek you,
and reveal yourself to me as I look for you.

**For I cannot seek you unless you first teach me,
not find you unless you first reveal yourself to me.**

St Ambrose (340–97)

Hymn

Choose one from the following:

I the Lord of sea and sky
Tell out my soul
We have a Gospel to proclaim

The blessing

Go out in the Love of God,
in the saving grace of Jesus our Saviour,
in the power and guidance of the Holy Spirit:
and the blessing of the Holy Trinity be upon you
and upon those whom you meet this day and always. **Amen**

Recollect

Take away with you a thought, a text or a resolution to use during the week. Always include in this a reminder of the presence and use it every day as often as possible.

Think on these words, and their response:

'"Whom shall I send, and who will go for us?" And I said, "Here am I; send me."' (Isaiah 6:8).

Continue to use the prayer of St Richard of Chichester from the previous chapter.

Resolve to seek to bring someone to a greater awareness of Jesus and his love.

Lent 4

The Samaritan woman at the well

Rest *(5 minutes)*

Imagine that you have been walking in the heat of the day. You have been on the road from early morning and now you are hot, tired and thirsty. It is has been a dry land you have been passing through with no refreshment. Life often feels like this. Perhaps as the day has heated up you feel a little dizzy or disorientated. Now you have come to a place of refreshment where you can rest. You have come to a place of cooling water. You do not have to do anything but enjoy being there. Relax and be at rest. Know that in the same way you have come to the presence of God and you are offered his love and peace.

Bringing all my burdens,
sorrow sin and care;
at thy feet I lay them
and I leave them there.

William Walsham How (1823–97)

Realise *(10 minutes)*

Say together the following:

We are in the grace, the goodness and the guidance of God, the Father, the Son and the Holy Spirit. Amen

Hymn
I heard the voice of Jesus say

Choose someone to lead you in the following:

Jesus says:

'Come to me, all you that are weary and are carrying heavy burdens, and I will give you rest' (Matthew 11:28).
The Lord is here.
His Spirit is with us.

'Let anyone who is thirsty come to me' (John 7:37).
The Lord is here.
His Spirit is with us.

'Those who drink of the water that I give them will never be thirsty' (John 4:14).
The Lord is here.
His Spirit is with us.

'My soul thirsts for God, for the living God' (Psalm 42:2).
The Lord is here.
His Spirit is with us.

O Lord our God, grant us grace
to desire you with our whole heart,
so that desiring you, we may seek and find you;
and so finding you, may love you;
and so love you, may hate those sins
which separate us from you,
for the sake of Jesus Christ our Lord.

St Anselm (1033–1109)

Blessed are you, Father, Son and Holy Spirit.
You have created us out of your love and for your love.
You have made our hearts to long for you
and nothing else will fully satisfy them.
Help us to turn to you in our hunger and thirst,
that in you we may find refreshment and life.
You, Lord, are the giver of life in all its fullness.
Blessed are you, Father, Son and Holy Spirit.

As the deer longs for flowing streams,
so longs my soul for you, O God.
My soul thirsts for God, for the living God.
When shall I come and behold the face of God? (Psalm 42:1-2).

Read *(10 minutes)*

John 4:1-42

Now when Jesus learned that the Pharisees had heard, 'Jesus is making and baptising more disciples than John' – ²although it was not Jesus himself but his disciples who baptised – ³he left Judea and started back to Galilee. ⁴But he had to go through Samaria. ⁵So he came to a Samaritan city called Sychar, near the plot of ground that Jacob had given to his son Joseph. ⁶Jacob's well was there, and Jesus, tired out by his journey, was sitting by the well. It was about noon.

⁷A Samaritan woman came to draw water, and Jesus said to her, 'Give me a drink.' ⁸(His disciples had gone to the city to buy food.) ⁹The Samaritan woman said to him, 'How is it that you, a Jew, ask a drink of me, a woman of Samaria?' (Jews do not share things in common with Samaritans.) ¹⁰Jesus answered her, 'If you knew the gift of God, and who it is that is saying to you, "Give me a drink", you would have asked him, and he would have given you living water.' ¹¹The woman said to him, 'Sir, you have no bucket, and the well is deep. Where do you get that living water? ¹²Are you greater than our ancestor Jacob, who gave us the well, and with his sons and his flocks drank from it?' ¹³Jesus said to her, 'Everyone who drinks of this water will be thirsty again, ¹⁴but those who drink of the water that I will give them will never be thirsty. The water that I will give will become in them a spring of water gushing up to eternal life.' ¹⁵The woman said to him, 'Sir, give me this water, so that I may never be thirsty or have to keep coming here to draw water.'

¹⁶Jesus said to her, 'Go, call your husband, and come back.' ¹⁷The woman answered him, 'I have no husband.' Jesus said to her, 'You are right in saying, "I have no husband"; ¹⁸for you have had five husbands, and the one you have now is not your husband. What you have said is true!' ¹⁹The woman said to him,

'Sir, I see that you are a prophet. [20]Our ancestors worshipped on this mountain, but you say that the place where people must worship is in Jerusalem.' [21]Jesus said to her, 'Woman, believe me, the hour is coming when you will worship the Father neither on this mountain nor in Jerusalem. [22]You worship what you do not know; we worship what we know, for salvation is from the Jews. [23]But the hour is coming, and is now here, when the true worshippers will worship the Father in spirit and truth, for the Father seeks such as these to worship him. [24]God is spirit, and those who worship him must worship in spirit and truth.' [25]The woman said to him, 'I know that Messiah is coming' (who is called Christ). 'When he comes, he will proclaim all things to us.' [26]Jesus said to her, 'I am he, the one who is speaking to you.'

[27]Just then his disciples came. They were astonished that he was speaking with a woman, but no one said, 'What do you want?' or, 'Why are you speaking with her?' [28]Then the woman left her water jar and went back to the city. She said to the people, [29]'Come and see a man who told me everything I have ever done! He cannot be the Messiah, can he?' [30]They left the city and were on their way to him.

[31]Meanwhile the disciples were urging him, 'Rabbi, eat something.' [32]But he said to them, 'I have food to eat that you do not know about.' [33]So the disciples said to one another, 'Surely no one has brought him something to eat?' [34]Jesus said to them, 'My food is to do the will of him who sent me and to complete his work. [35]Do you not say, "Four months more, then comes the harvest?" but I tell you, look around you, and see how the fields are ripe for harvesting. [36]The reaper is already receiving wages and is gathering fruit for eternal life, so that sower and reaper may rejoice together. [37]For here the saying holds true, "One sows and another reaps." [38]I sent you to reap that for which you did not labour. Others have laboured, and you have entered into their labour.'

[39]Many Samaritans from that city believed in him because of the woman's testimony, 'He told me everything I have ever done.' [40]So when the Samaritans came to him, they asked him to stay with them; and he stayed there two days. [41]And many more believed because of his word. [42]They said to the woman, 'It is no longer because of what you said that we believe, for we have

heard for ourselves, and we know that this is truly the Saviour of the world.'

Comments

Jesus and the disciples have left Judea on a three-day journey to Galilee. Palestine is 120 miles long and is divided into Judea in the south, Galilee in the north with Samaria in between. St John suggests Jesus 'had to go' through Samaria, yet there is an alternative route, though it would take twice as long. Perhaps John wants us to notice that this was a meeting that had to take place. Jesus was not for the Jews alone, but for all of humankind. This is a story that involves outreach in many ways. The setting is Jacob's well, a place full of history. Here was a piece of ground bought by Jacob (Genesis 33:18-19). On his death bed Jacob left this land to his son Joseph (Genesis 48:22). Then when Joseph died he was brought here for burial (Joshua 24:32).

The time is midday; the disciples have gone off to buy food from the Samaritans, which in itself indicates that Jesus had already influenced their attitude towards these people. The Jews described them as 'goy', that is alien: once they would not have approached Samaritans for food. Jesus is left alone at the well and he is thirsty. The well is about 100 feet deep and he has no means of drawing water. Jesus sees a Samaritan woman approach. Her thirst must be great to bring her out at midday – or perhaps she had hoped not to meet anyone. She is amazed that Jesus speaks to her. A rabbi was not allowed to speak to a woman in public – not even to his wife or daughter – so Jesus was risking his reputation. As the story unwinds it gets worse. Not only is this a woman but also a Samaritan, and Jews have no dealings with Samaritans (v9). Then to make matters worse the woman is amoral or immoral. Would the Son of God be found here, with such a woman? No wonder the disciples would like to have asked, 'What are you doing with her.' It is quite natural that she leaves as they arrive.

Ruminate *(in silence 5 minutes, shared 5 minutes)*

Picture the conversation at the well. Try and visualise the delicate relationship, and how both are careful in their dealings. Remember the barriers of male and female, Jew and Samaritan, a 'holy man' and an immoral woman. Note how they are not barriers to Jesus.

Be aware of the progress, the woman has called Jesus 'a Jew', 'Sir', 'a prophet' and now asks if he can be 'the Messiah'. She speaks of what she has personally experienced, and not of some theory. She has met the living Lord. Now she wants to witness to him, to share her experience.

What is the name you would give to Jesus? Is he more to you than a teacher or an example? Choose a name to bring to the group that expresses your relationship with Jesus.

As a group

Begin by allowing each individual to say what title or name they would give Jesus.

Because of the woman, the Samaritans came to Jesus. They asked him to stay and he stayed with them two days. They believed in him when they heard him. They said 'we have heard for ourselves, and we know that this is truly the Saviour of the world' (v42). Others may seek to bring us to Christ but we have to make our own contact. Jesus is not just a teacher, a prophet, an example or a friend he is the Saviour of the world (see John 3:16). Jesus is not exclusive to the Jews or the Samaritans but for everyone. There is a progression from no faith (4:1-15), to partial faith: 'can this be the Messiah' (4:16-30), to the authentic faith of the Samaritans' first-hand experience (4:39-42).

Let each give ideas about how we learn to abide with Jesus and let him abide with us.

If time permits, you may like to look at the following:
How do we show that Jesus accepts all who come to him?

In what ways are we given the opportunity to grow in the faith?

How are new Christians nurtured and cared for in our faith community?

React *(directed to God 5 minutes, shared with the group 10 minutes)*

Read the following sentences to yourself and give thanks that God loves us, seeks us and calls us. Know that often our emptiness is a sign that we have ignored the living God.

'No one has ever called upon him without first having been called by him.'

Augustine of Hippo (354–430)

The Samaritan woman could not have thirsted for God unless God was thirsting for her and her love. 'No one can come to me unless drawn by the Father who sent me' (John 6:44).

'It is you who have aroused this desire in us because you made us for yourself, and our hearts are restless until they rest in you.'

Augustine of Hippo

'Through our Lord Jesus Christ . . . you came to seek us, who did not seek you, and you sought us, so that we might seek you.'

Augustine of Hippo

As a group

Now take it in turns to read the sentences above out loud and then discuss ways in which we reveal our thirst for God. Give each other a chance to express how you feel about the passage you have all read.

Rest and rejoice *(in silence for 2 minutes, final prayers, music and blessing 5–8 minutes)*

In the silence realise how much you need God to live life to the full. Rejoice in the power of your Saviour to refresh and renew you. You may like to say:

Lord Jesus Christ, my Saviour
I come to you in my emptiness:
I, who hunger and thirst, come to you.
I who can perish in the wilderness
come to you for hope and for help.
I come for refreshment, for renewal, for strength.
I come to you for your love and your presence.
I come to you for in you is eternal life.
You are the true and life-giving stream:
you are the Word of Life, Christ my Lord.

Final prayers and music
Choose someone to lead you in the following:

To our emptiness Jesus comes.
To our weariness Jesus comes.
Praise to Christ our Saviour.

To our hunger Jesus comes.
To our boredom Jesus comes.
Praise to Christ our Saviour.

To all who are perishing Jesus comes.
To all who thirst for God, Jesus comes.
Praise to Christ our Saviour.

He comes to nourish us and strengthen us.
He comes to be with us and give us life eternal.
Praise to Christ our Saviour.

Lord Jesus, our Saviour, let us now come to you.
Our hearts are cold; Lord, warm them with your selfless love.
Our hearts are sinful; cleanse them with your precious blood.
Our hearts are weak; strengthen them with your joyous Spirit.
Our hearts are empty; fill them with your divine presence.
Lord Jesus, our hearts are yours, possess them always.

Augustine of Hippo (354–430)

Hymn

Choose one from the following list:

Jesu, thou joy of loving hearts
There's a wideness in God's mercy
Have you heard the raindrops?

The blessing

The Lord Jesus come to you and
fill your emptiness with his presence,
fill your loneliness with his love,
fill your sadness with his joy,
fill you with the grace and goodness of God:
and the blessing of God Almighty,
the Father, the Son and the Holy Spirit
be upon you and remain with you always. **Amen**

Recollect

Take away with you a thought, a text or a resolution to use
during the week. Always include in this a reminder of the
presence and use it every day as often as possible.

You may like to learn these words and think over them
this week:

'It is you who have aroused this desire in us because you
made us for yourself, and our hearts are restless until they
rest in you.'

Augustine of Hippo

You may also like to use these words:

'The Lord is my shepherd, I shall not want.
He makes me lie down in green pastures;
he leads me beside still waters;
he restores my soul' (Psalm 23:1-3).

Lent 5

I once was blind but now I see

Rest *(5 minutes)*

In our desire for speed we often fail to see what is around us. We do not look long enough or deep enough at the beauty of the world. We need to look with the eyes of our heart at what is around us. We need to teach ourselves to give people and the world our full attention. So stop all hurrying and relax: enjoy the quietness of this time. Make sure your body is free of tensions. Again, check it over from head to foot and tell it to relax. Still your mind by giving it something beautiful to look at. Give thanks for your ability to see. Rejoice in the beauty of a flower, of a scene or of a person.

Realise *(10 minutes)*

Say together:

We are in the light and love of the Lord, Father, Son and Holy Spirit.

Hymn

Open our eyes Lord, we want to see Jesus

Choose someone to lead you in the following:

Open our eyes, Lord, to your presence.
The Lord is here.
His Spirit is with us.

Open our hearts, Lord, to your love.
The Lord is here.
His Spirit is with us.

Open our ears, Lord, to your call.
The Lord is here.
His Spirit is with us.

Open our lives, Lord, to your presence.
The Lord is here.
His Spirit is with us.

Blessed are you Lord God of all creation,
by your love you have created the world
in light and in beauty.
You have given us so much to delight our eyes
Lord touch our lives,
scattering the darkness from our hearts and minds,
opening our eyes to the beauty around us
and to the wonder of your presence and love.
Blessed are you Father, Son and Holy Spirit.

O Lord, the Word, O God the Word,
you are light and through you light was made . . .
light, without whom is only darkness.
Way, aside from whom is only error.
Truth, without whom is only vanity.
Life without whom is only death.
Speak a word, say O Lord,
'Let there be light'
that I may avoid the darkness,
see the way and avoid false steps,
see the truth and avoid vanity,
see life and avoid death.
Give me light, O Lord my light,
my splendour and my salvation . . .
Give light, O Light,
to this blind servant of yours
who sits in darkness and in the shadow of death,
and guide his feet into the way of peace.
St Augustine of Hippo (354–430)

May the glorious Christ our Saviour
scatter the darkness from our hearts and minds
and from this world.

Read *(10 minutes)*

John 9:1-41

¹As he walked along, he saw a man blind from birth. ²His disciples asked him, 'Rabbi, who sinned, this man or his parents, that he was born blind?' ³Jesus answered, 'Neither this man nor his parents sinned; he was born blind so that God's works might be revealed in him. ⁴We must work the works of him who sent me while it is day; night is coming when no one can work. ⁵As long as I am in the world, I am the light of the world.' ⁶When he had said this, he spat on the ground and made mud with the saliva and spread the mud on the man's eyes, ⁷saying to him, 'Go, wash in the pool of Siloam' (which means Sent). Then he went and washed and came back able to see. ⁸The neighbours and those who had seen him before as a beggar began to ask, 'Is this not the man who used to sit and beg?' ⁹Some were saying, 'It is he.' Others were saying, 'No, but it is someone like him.' He kept saying, 'I am the man.' ¹⁰But they kept asking him, 'Then how were your eyes opened?' ¹¹He answered, 'The man called Jesus made mud, spread it on my eyes, and said to me, "Go to Siloam and wash." Then I went and washed and received my sight.' ¹²They said to him, 'Where is he?' he said, 'I do not know.'

¹³They brought to the Pharisees the man who had formerly been blind. ¹⁴Now it was a sabbath day when Jesus made the mud and opened his eyes. ¹⁵Then the Pharisees also began to ask him how he had received his sight. He said to them, 'He put mud on my eyes. Then I washed, and now I see.' ¹⁶Some of the Pharisees said, 'This man is not from God, for he does not observe the sabbath.' But others said, 'How can a man who is a sinner perform such signs?' And they were divided. ¹⁷So they said again to the blind man, 'What do you say about him? It was your eyes he opened.' He said, 'He is a prophet.'

¹⁸The Jews did not believe that he had been blind and had received his sight until they called the parents of the man who

had received his sight [19]and asked them, 'Is this your son, who you say was born blind? How then does he now see?' [20]His parents answered, 'We know that this is our son, and that he was born blind; [21]but we do not know how it is that now he sees, nor do we know who opened his eyes. Ask him; he is of age. He will speak for himself.' [22]His parents said this because they were afraid of the Jews; for the Jews had already agreed that anyone who confessed Jesus to be the Messiah would be put out of the synagogue. [23]Therefore his parents said, 'He is of age; ask him.'

[24]So for the second time they called the man who had been blind, and they said to him, 'Give glory to God! We know that this man is a sinner.' [25]He answered, 'I do not know whether he is a sinner. One thing I do know, that though I was blind, now I see.' [26]They said to him, 'What did he do to you? How did he open your eyes?' [27]He answered them, 'I have told you already, and you would not listen. Why do you want to hear it again? Do you also want to become his disciples?' [28]Then they reviled him, saying, 'You are his disciple, but we are disciples of Moses. [29]We know that God has spoken to Moses, but as for this man, we do not know where he comes from.' [30]The man answered, 'Here is an astonishing thing! You do not know where he comes from, and yet he opened my eyes. [31]We know that God does not listen to sinners, but he does listen to one who worships him and obeys his will. [32]Never since the world began has it been heard that anyone opened the eyes of a person born blind. [33]If this man were not from God, he could do nothing.' [34]They answered him, 'You were born entirely in sin, and are you trying to teach us?' And they drove him out.

[35]Jesus heard that they had driven him out, and when he found him, he said, 'Do you believe in the Son of Man?' [36]He answered, 'And who is he, sir? Tell me, so that I may believe in him.' [37]Jesus said to him, 'You have seen him, and the one speaking with you is he.' [38]He said, 'Lord, I believe.' And he worshipped him. [39]Jesus said, 'I came into this world for judgement so that those who do not see may see, and those who do see may become blind.' [40]Some of the Pharisees near him heard this and said to him, 'Surely we are not blind, are we?' [41]Jesus said to them, 'If you were blind, you would not have sin. But now that you say, "We see," your sin remains.'

Comments

Jesus and the disciples (9:1-5)

It is the Sabbath day; Jesus has come from the Temple and is passing by a man that has been blind from birth. This is the only sufferer in the Gospels who is afflicted from birth. The disciples want to align suffering with sin and ask 'who sinned this man or his parents?' As God should not be credited with the evils that befall us who should be blamed? Rather than theorise about the cause, Jesus tells them it is an opportunity to show what God can do (v3). The disciples are included in this saving work (v4). In John's Gospel miracles are always a sign of power and glory. Jesus declares he is the Light of the World (v5, see also 1:4-9, 8:12).

Jesus and the man born blind (9:6-7)

Jesus, the Light of the world, will now bring light to this man who lives in darkness. In using spittle to make mud Jesus uses a traditional practise. It was believed that spittle had curative properties. Though the man could not see he was aware of the presence and the actions. He is told to go and wash his eyes in the pool of Siloam. He obeyed and came back seeing.

The blind man and his neighbours (9:8-12)

People found it hard to believe; how was it possible? Who did this thing? The man has to insist he is the man who was blind. He tells them the man called Jesus has given him sight. They ask where Jesus is but he does not know.

The blind man and the Pharisees (9:13-17)

The Pharisees do not see the miracle as much as an offence. They are more interested in keeping their traditions than seeing the wonder that has been performed. Jesus has failed to observe the Sabbath in the making of mud and anointing the man's eyes. He cannot be from God because he does not keep the Sabbath. But others were saying can a sinner perform such signs? There was a division among the people. So the Pharisees ask the man born blind what do you say. He replies, 'He is a prophet.'

The blind man's parents and the Pharisees (9:18-23)

The Pharisees refuse to see! They did not believe that sight had been restored to a blind man. So, now the parents of the man born blind are interrogated. Yes he is their son. Yes he was born blind. But beyond this they refused to be drawn, because they were afraid, as the Jews had already agreed that anyone who confesses Jesus to be the Messiah would be put out of the synagogue. They get out of it by suggesting the Pharisees ask the man himself.

The blind man and the Pharisees again (9:24-34)

The interrogation turns again to the man born blind. They ask him to praise God, not Jesus for he is a sinner. The man replies that he does not know if Jesus is a sinner, he only knows he once was blind but now he sees. Again they ask what did Jesus do to him. They are stuck with 'how' and they do not want to acknowledge 'who'. They will analyse this but come no closer to Jesus. Then the man asks, why, when they have refused to hear, do they want to hear again? Do they want to become disciples? For this statement they revile the man. Yet the man knows what has happened to him, he stands his ground. He declares Jesus is from God. The Pharisees are unwilling to acknowledge what is said. For this the man is driven out. In the same way they will drive Jesus out of their lives.

The blind man and Jesus (9:35-38)

Jesus finds the man: so often when we cannot find our God he seeks us out and finds us. Jesus asks him, 'Do you believe in the Son of Man?' (v35). The man asks, 'And who is he, sir?' (v36). Jesus tells him 'The one speaking to you is he' (v37). The man replies, 'Lord, I believe' (v38). And he worshipped him. Note the progress, he has called Jesus 'a man', 'a prophet', 'Sir' then 'Lord'. He bows before Jesus who has opened his eyes and the eyes of his heart. Jesus is the One who makes God known, he is the Son of Man, the Sent one, the Light of the World. What Jesus said in John 9:3 is now fulfilled.

Jesus and the Pharisees (9:39-41)

Jesus talks of 'judgement', which comes about by his coming into the world. He does not condemn but shows the Pharisees for what they are. The coming of Jesus is always a time of opportunity or the loss of opportunity. His presence opens eyes to him and to a fuller life. But many who say they see fail to do so. The person who is conscious of his own blindness has a far better chance of seeing than those who think they know it all.

Ruminate *(in silence 5 minutes, shared 5 minutes)*

Visualise yourself in the position of the blind man: dwell on the amazing fact that you can now see. Why are the authorities not able to see this? How does Jesus open your eyes to a fuller life?

As a group

Pick out the highlights of this story as if you are making a film. Start with the blind man before Jesus and think about how to capture his joy. Look at the reaction of Pharisees to the man, his parents and to Jesus. End with Jesus talking about seeing and blindness.

Give everyone a chance to say how Jesus opens their eyes to what life is truly about.

React *(directed to God 5 minutes, shared with the group 10 minutes)*

Give Jesus your love (worship) by thinking on his various titles and affirming his presence as you sit in the quiet:

Jesus, Son of God: open my eyes to your presence, my heart to your love.

Jesus, Son of Man: open my eyes to your presence, my heart to your love.

Jesus, Light of the world: open my eyes to your presence, my heart to your love.

Jesus, Prince of peace: open my eyes to your presence, my heart to your love.

Jesus, Christ my Saviour: open my eyes to your presence, my heart to your love.

It may be hard to define what you mean when you call Jesus 'Christ' or 'Saviour' but every so often you should seek to deepen the meaning of these words: ask yourself what you mean.

As a group

You may like to think more about the progress in the blind man's insight as he calls Jesus 'a man', then 'a prophet', then 'Sir'. He tells Jesus he believes that he is the 'Son of Man' and worships him calling him 'Lord'. Do you see your faith as something that grows and progresses through your relationship with Jesus?

'I was blind, now I see.' Seek to portray the emotions, the wonder and joy of this statement. Let each member of the group add to how they think the blind man felt.

Do we realise how blind we are unless we allow Jesus to touch us?

Discuss one or more of these and then give each person a chance to share their responses to this passage.

Rest and rejoice (*in silence for 2 minutes, final prayers, music and blessing 5–8 minutes*)
Use this prayer within the quietness to affirm the presence of Jesus with you now.

Come my Lord, my Light, my Way,
come, be known to me this day.
Come open my eyes that I may see
your presence and light all about me.
Come O Christ, with love to my heart:
with me abide and never depart.

Final prayers and music
Choose someone to lead you in the following:

Thou, who didst come to bring
on thy redeeming wing,
healing and sight,
health to the sick in mind,
sight to the inly blind,
O now to all mankind
let there be light.

John Marriott (1780–1825)

O Lord God we thank you for the gift of sight
and for insight,
for the ability to be aware of you and your love.
Help us to see that you are with us always
and to see your presence in those we meet.
Touch our eyes that we do not lose this vision,
Jesus Christ our Lord. **Amen**

O God, you are the light of the minds that know you,
the life of the souls that love you,
and the strength of the wills that serve you:
help us so to know you, that we may truly love you,

and so to love you that we may fully serve you,
whose service is perfect freedom,
through Jesus Christ our Lord. **Amen**

Augustine of Hippo (354-430)

Hymn

Choose one of the following:

Amazing grace how sweet the sound
Lord the light of your love is shining
Thou whose almighty word

The blessing

The Lord God, open your eyes to his presence,
open you heart to his love,
open your life to his light:
and the blessing of God Almighty,
the Father, the Son and the Holy Spirit
be upon you this day and ever more. **Amen**

Recollect

Take away with you a thought, a text or a resolution to use
during the week. Always include in this a reminder of the
presence and use it every day as often as possible.

I have given a suggested prayer below:

Lord, that I may receive my sight:
open my eyes to your presence, my heart to your love.

Repeat this prayer during the week, sometimes replacing
'Lord' with another title given to Jesus.

Continue to use the prayer of St Richard of Chichester
from chapter 2.

Lent 6

The Greeks: We would see Jesus

Rest *(5 minutes)*

In our busyness we allow so much to crowd out the presence of our Lord. We have full days and surround ourselves with sound. Even when we come to prayer our minds are still racing. Seek to be still in body and mind. Relax your body, checking it over from head to feet. Rest in the presence of Jesus and offer him your love. Every time your mind strays bring it back to Jesus with the words, 'We would see Jesus.' Rejoice in his friendship and the fact that he never leaves you.

Realise *(10 minutes)*

Say together:

We are in the grace and goodness of God, Father, Son and Holy Spirit.

Hymn

I heard the voice of Jesus say

Choose someone to lead you in the following:

'Where two or three are gathered in my name, I am there among them' (Matthew 18:20).
The Lord is here.
His Spirit is with us.

'Whoever welcomes one such child in my name welcomes me' (Matthew 18:5).
The Lord is here.
His Spirit is with us.

'I heard the voice of the Lord saying, "Whom shall I send,
and who will go for us?" And I said, "Here am I; send me"'
(Isaiah 6:8).
The Lord is here.
His Spirit is with us.

'Go therefore and make disciples of all nations, baptising
them in the name of the Father and of the Son and of the
Holy Spirit' (Matthew 28:19).
The Lord is here.
His Spirit is with us.

'Remember, I am with you always' (Matthew 28:20).
The Lord is here.
His Spirit is with us.

Blessed are you, Lord our God,
for you have called us to know you and to love you.
Lord, as we draw close to you,
help us to know you better,
and in knowing you, love you more
and in loving you, draw others to your love
that they also may rejoice in seeing and loving you.
Blessed are you Father, Son and Holy Spirit.

Lord God, you have made us one in you
and one with each other in a common unity of love.
Help us to avoid all that divides us and separates us
from each other and from you.
Let us make sure we never make it difficult for
others to come to you.
As you have called us in love
may we reveal that love and draw others to you.
We ask this in the love of him who was lifted up for us,
our Saviour, Jesus Christ. **Amen**

Read *(10 minutes)*

John 12:20-26

> [20]Now among those who went up to worship at the festival were some Greeks. [21]They came to Philip, who was from Bethsaida in Galilee, and said to him, 'Sir, we wish to see Jesus.' [22]Philip went and told Andrew; then Andrew and Philip went and told Jesus. [23]Jesus answered them, 'The hour has come for the Son of Man to be glorified. [24]Very truly, I tell you, unless a grain of wheat falls into the earth and dies, it remains just a single grain; but if it dies, it bears much fruit. [25]Those who love their life lose it, and those who hate their life in this world will keep it for eternal life. [26]Whoever serves me must follow me, and where I am, there will my servant be also. Whoever serves me, the Father will honour.'

Comments

In the verses before our passage we learn that it is coming up to Passover time in Jerusalem. The chief priests and Pharisees are seeking to arrest Jesus (11:57). Jesus stays at the home of Lazarus and there Mary anoints his feet (12:1-8). Because of the crowd coming to see Lazarus and Jesus, the chief priests plan to put Lazarus as well as Jesus to death (12:9-11). Jesus rides into Jerusalem on a donkey and is welcomed by a crowd shouting praise (12:12-18). The popular demonstrations alarm the authorities. The Pharisees despair saying to one another, 'You see, you can do nothing. Look, the world has gone after him' (12:19).

In John 12:20-22 there is a sense that these words are fulfilled by the 'non-Jews' that seek Jesus. Among those who have come up to the festival to worship are some Greeks. The other three Gospels do not record the coming of the Greeks to Jesus. As John's Gospel was written in a way to present it to the Greek-speaking community it is fitting the Greeks should find they are included among those who come to Jesus.

An awareness of Jesus has reached out far beyond the Jews now. He met with the Samaritans who believed in him (John 4:39-42), and he is about to meet the Gentiles who had already heard something about him. The Greeks approach Philip, possibly because of his Greek name. They say, 'Sir, we wish to see Jesus.' In St John's Gospel, seeing is paralleled with 'believing'. Philip tells Andrew, who came from Bethsaida, the same town as Philip (1:44), and is the only other disciple whose name comes to us in its Greek form. Andrew and Philip go together to tell Jesus. The reaction of Jesus when he learns the Greeks want to meet him is to say, 'The hour has come for the Son of Man to be glorified' (v23). This sentence must have brought joy to the hearts of the disciples: 'glory' is good to have. But they did not as yet understand the glory Jesus was talking about. This is actually crisis time – and crisis is a time of judgement and of opportunity (see 1:51, 3:14, 8:28, 12:34). It is a time when he is accepted or rejected and both are going on around Jesus all the time. The 'Church', which is the main officials, the chief priests and Pharisees, are against him while at the same time we hear how Samaritans and Greeks accept him. Jesus realises his death is not far away. He talks of how a grain of wheat must be buried to rise again. Through death comes life. How often this has been true for the Church: Tertullian in the third century said, 'The blood of the martyrs is the seed of the Church.' The glory Jesus talks about is not about power, conquest or rule but about power gained through giving and loving.

'Whoever serves me must follow me, and where I am there will my servant be also' (v26). Following Jesus sounds grand but it is the way of the cross. When it comes, for a while even his disciples deserted him. We are privileged to know more than the disciples for we know that beyond the cross is the resurrection. We know what Jesus says is true: 'I know them and they follow me. I will give them eternal life, and they will never perish' (John 10: 27-8).

Ruminate *(in silence 5 minutes, shared 5 minutes)*

Quietly picture the Greeks approaching the disciples and their coming to Jesus. What do you think drew them to him? How would they feel standing before him?

We are not told much about them. It could be they were sightseers interested in the festival, or travellers curious just to learn more of this person so many were talking about. Note it does say they came up to worship. They may have been caught up in the excitement of the entry of Jesus into Jerusalem. The important element of the story is that they are presented as Gentiles from another country. It is unlikely that they knew much about the Scriptures or about the Christ but that is not a barrier. The love of God does not set us a test before we are allowed to come into his presence: he accepts us as we are. He is aware of our potential and our ability to change. He does not seek knowledge from books so much as a relationship with him. When seeking Jesus for ourselves or when bringing people to Jesus we should remember his words, 'Anyone who comes to me I will never drive away' (John 6:37). There is no moment like the present to come to him. Do this now.

In the quiet say:

And I come, O Jesus:
dare I turn away?
No, thy love hath conquered,
and I come today.

Bringing all my burdens,
sorrow sin and care;
at thy feet I lay them,
and I leave them there.

William Walsham How (1823–97)

As a group

Think about the fact that more people are brought to Jesus through the witness and example of someone else than by reading. We are all called to share in the outreach and mission of Jesus. It is by sharing the Good News, by introducing people to Jesus, that the Church grows and survives. This is not the work of a few; it is the work of us all. There can be nothing more wonderful you can do for people: remember just bringing them to church is not necessarily bringing them to Jesus. You need be sure they 'see Jesus'.

Give all the opportunity to say when they last brought someone to Jesus.

Here are some other discussion starters you can use if you have time:

If you do not talk to Christ can you truly love him?
If you do not talk of Christ do you really appreciate what he has done?
Is it not wrong to keep the Lord to ourselves?
A faith not shared is not likely to grow.

React *(directed to God 5 minutes, shared with the group 10 minutes)*

Charles Simeon, leading evangelical and one of the founders of the Church Missionary Society, was the vicar of Holy Trinity Church in Cambridge. He had carved inside the pulpit the words from John 12:21, 'Sir, we would see Jesus' to serve as a constant reminder that the people did not come to gaze at a great preacher but to be brought to see and know Jesus personally. The task of all preachers is to let people see Jesus.

In the quiet, come before Jesus. Give thanks for those who have brought you to an awareness of Jesus, for all who have been an influence on your Christian life.

Pray for those around you who do not know Jesus.

Pray that you may have the privilege of bringing them to Jesus.

As a group

Give each one a chance to say what struck them most about the passage.

Discuss how the Church can present the living Lord better, so that people may see him and know him.

Do we have attitudes and traditions that do not help people to see Jesus?

Each make a promise to try and bring someone to a deeper awareness of Jesus.

Rest and rejoice (*in silence for 2 minutes, final prayers, music and blessing 5–8 minutes*)

Be still in the presence of our Lord. Rejoice that he welcomes you and enfolds you in his love.

Pray quietly to yourself:

Lord, as you enfold us all in your love,
use me to reveal your love
and to share your love
with those around me.
Lord, show me
how to bring others to you
and use me as you will,
Christ my Saviour.

Final prayers and music

Choose someone to lead you in the following:

Lord, as you draw near to us,
we draw near to you,
to be aware of your presence,
to rest in your love,
to learn of your saving power.

As we abide with you
enable us to draw others to you
and by our words, our example,
our way of living, show
them your great love, Christ our Lord.

God, bless your Church
that it may grow in love for you,
seek to proclaim your presence
and reveal your glory to the world.
Bless all who through their lives
bring others to any awareness of you
by their lives and witness.

We ask your guidance on ministers of the Word
and the sacraments,
and ourselves involved in your mission.
We ask this in your love, Jesus Christ our Lord. **Amen**

Hymn

Pick one to sing together:

O my Saviour lifted
Lord Jesus Christ you have come to us
Lord of all hopefulness

The blessing

The love of God, our Father, empower you:
the light of Christ, our Saviour, radiate in your life:
the leading of the Holy Spirit guide you:
that you may draw others to the glory, grace and goodness
of the Holy and blessed Trinity:
and the blessing of God Almighty, the Father, the Son
and the Holy Spirit
be upon you now and always. **Amen**

Recollect

Take away with you a thought, a text or a resolution to use during the week. Always include in this a reminder of the presence and use it every day as often as possible. Try to pray at the beginning of each day 'I would see Jesus' and also look out for opportunities to proclaim his presence.

You may like to pray each day:

All this day, O Lord,
let me touch as many lives as possible for thee:
and every life I touch, do thou by thy Spirit quicken,
whether through the word I speak,
the prayer I breathe or the life I live.

Mary Sumner (1828–1921)

Easter

Mary Magdalene: I have seen the Lord
Thomas: Blessed are those who have not seen and yet have believed

Rest *(5 minutes)*

Too often we fail to give attention to the people we are with. In the same way we ignore the presence of our Lord: slow down so you can rest now in his presence. Enjoy this time with the risen Lord and let his light and love conquer any fear or darkness that is about you. If your mind wanders bring it back with the reminder, 'the risen Lord is here with me'.

Realise *(10 minutes)*

Say together:

We are in the love and the light of the Lord, Father, Son and Holy Spirit.

Hymn

Jesus these eyes have never seen

Light a candle to remind the group of the presence of risen Lord. Choose someone to lead you in the following:

Alleluia! Christ is risen.
He is risen indeed. Alleluia!

May Christ, risen in glory,
scatter the darkness from our hearts,
from our minds and from this world.

'Mary Magdalene went and said to the disciples "I have seen the Lord"' (John 20:18).
The Lord is here.
His Spirit is with us.

'Then the disciples rejoiced when they saw the Lord' (John 20:20).
The Lord is here.
His Spirit is with us.

'Jesus said . . . "have you believed because you have seen me?"' (John 20:29).
The Lord is here.
His Spirit is with us.

'Blessed are those who have not seen and yet have come to believe' (John 20:29).
The Lord is here.
His Spirit is with us.

'Everyone who lives and believes in me will never die' (John 11:26).
The Lord is here.
His Spirit is with us.

Blessed are you, Lord our God,
to you be praise and glory for ever.
In the glorious resurrection of our Lord Jesus Christ
you have led us to freedom:
through him light conquers darkness,
love defeats hatred,
life triumphs over death.
In him we have life eternal.
Blessed are you Father, Son and Holy Spirit.

Lord Jesus Christ,
you made yourself known after your resurrection

to Mary Magdalene in the garden,
to the disciples inside a house,
to Thomas in his doubting:
come and be known among us.
Fill our emptiness with your presence:
fill our darkness with your light
fill our doubt with your loving touch.
Let us know you are here with us now and always,
Christ our Lord conqueror of death. **Amen**

Read *(10 minutes)*

John 20:1-31

[1]Early on the first day of the week, while it was still dark, Mary Magdalene came to the tomb and saw that the stone had been removed from the tomb. [2]So she ran and went to Simon Peter and the other disciple, the one whom Jesus loved, and said to them, 'They have taken the Lord out of the tomb, and we do not know where they have laid him.' [3]Then Peter and the other disciple set out and went toward the tomb. [4]The two were running together, but the other disciple outran Peter and reached the tomb first. [5]He bent down to look in and saw the linen wrappings lying there, but he did not go in. [6]Then Simon Peter came, following him, and went into the tomb. He saw the linen wrappings lying there, [7]and the cloth that had been on Jesus' head, not lying with the linen wrappings but rolled up in a place by itself. [8]Then the other disciple, who reached the tomb first, also went in, and he saw and believed; [9]for as yet they did not understand the scripture, that he must rise from the dead. [10]Then the disciples returned to their homes.

[11]But Mary stood weeping outside the tomb. As she wept, she bent over to look into the tomb; [12]and she saw two angels in white, sitting where the body of Jesus had been lying, one at the head and the other at the feet. [13]They said to her, 'Woman, why are you weeping?' She said to them, 'They have taken away my Lord, and I do not know where they have laid him.' [14]When she had said this, she turned around and saw Jesus standing there, but she did not know that it was Jesus. [15]Jesus said to her, 'Woman, why are you weeping? Whom are you looking for?'

Supposing him to be the gardener, she said to him, 'Sir, if you have carried him away, tell me where you have laid him, and I will take him away.' [16]Jesus said to her, 'Mary!' She turned and said to him in Hebrew, 'Rabbouni!' (which means Teacher). [17]Jesus said to her, 'Do not hold on to me, because I have not yet ascended to the Father. But go to my brothers and say to them, "I am ascending to my Father and your Father, to my God and your God."' [18]Mary Magdalene went and announced to the disciples, 'I have seen the Lord'; and she told them that he had said these things to her.

[19]When it was evening on that day, the first day of the week and the doors of the house where the disciples had met were locked for fear of the Jews, Jesus came and stood among them and said, 'Peace be with you.' [20]After he said this, he showed them his hands and his side. Then the disciples rejoiced when they saw the Lord. [21]Jesus said to them again, 'Peace be with you. As the Father has sent me, so I send you.' [22]When he had said this, he breathed on them and said to them, 'Receive the Holy Spirit. [23]If you forgive the sins of any, they are forgiven them; if you retain the sins of any, they are retained.' [24]But Thomas (who was called the Twin), one of the twelve, was not with them when Jesus came. [25]So the other disciples told him, 'We have seen the Lord.' But he said to them, 'Unless I see the mark of the nails in his hands, and put my finger in the mark of the nails and my hand in his side, I will not believe.'

[26]A week later his disciples were again in the house, and Thomas was with them. Although the doors were shut, Jesus came and stood among them and said, 'Peace be with you.' [27]Then he said to Thomas, 'Put your finger here and see my hands. Reach out your hand and put it in my side. Do not doubt but believe.' [28]Thomas answered him, 'My Lord and my God!' [29]Jesus said to him, 'Have you believed because you have seen me? Blessed are those who have not seen and yet have come to believe.'

[30]Now Jesus did many other signs in the presence of his disciples, which are not written in this book. [31]But these are written so that you may come to believe that Jesus is the Messiah, the Son of God, and that through believing you may have life in his name.

Comments

First reactions (21:1-2)

In these verses we learn that it is the 'first day of the week', Sunday. It is early in the day, between three and six. Mary goes to the tomb to pay her respects at the grave only to discover the stone that sealed it had been removed. Her immediate reaction is to run from the place and to tell Simon Peter and the other disciple, the one whom Jesus loved. It is thought that this second disciple could be young John, the author of the Gospel. Mary has seen the empty tomb but it only makes her think of grave robbers, as Jesus is, as far as she is concerned, dead.

The empty tomb (v3-10)

In these verses we see Peter and John run to the tomb. As John is a young man he outruns Peter. He sees the linen wrappings inside but does not go in. Peter goes into the tomb and sees the linen wrappings and the cloth that had wrapped the head in place by itself. John now enters and sees the wrappings and immediately believes something wonderful has happened. They then leave for home.

Mary and the risen Lord (v11-18)

Mary has returned and stands outside the tomb weeping. She looks into the tomb and sees two angels in white, one at the head and the other at the feet of where Jesus had been lying. They ask, 'Woman why are you weeping?' Mary can still only think that the body has been removed by 'someone'. Then she is aware of someone behind her. In the half light of day with tears in her eyes, she assumes him to be the gardener. Mary says, 'Sir, if you have carried him away, tell me where you have laid him, and I will take him away.' Jesus says to her 'Mary!' Only now does she fully turn to him and says 'Rabbouni'.

It would seem Mary embraces her Lord. It is so good for her to be with him again that all the sorrow and all the loss is gone. But she cannot keep the news to herself alone. This is far more important than the empty tomb or folded grave clothes. Jesus lives! The meeting with the living Lord is an encounter that must be told, needs to be shared. Jesus says, 'Do not hold on to me, but go and tell my brothers.' She returns to the disciples and announces, 'I have seen the Lord.' We are not told of the disciples' reaction; perhaps they doubted Mary.

Joy and new life (v19-23)

The scene now moves to the evening. The disciples have gathered, though Judas is absent and Thomas is not with them. The doors are locked because of fear of the Jews. Jesus stands among them and says, 'Peace be with you.' He shows them the nail holes and where the spear had torn his side. Jesus is alive! He is not a ghost, he has a body and it has the scars of the crucifixion. A great joy fills the disciples' hearts. As God breathed life into the first humans, and the Spirit of God gave life to the dry bones, Jesus breathes new life into his disciples. He gives them the Holy Spirit and commissions them to forgive or retain sins.

Thomas wants to see for himself (v24-5)

Sometime after this Thomas arrives. The disciples tell him, 'We have seen the Lord.' Thomas refuses to believe unless he can experience this for himself. He wants to see for himself.

Believing without seeing (v26-9)

Seeing cannot occur simply on demand. A week later when they were again gathered together behind closed doors Jesus comes once more. Thomas is invited to touch and see for himself. Jesus says, 'Do not doubt but believe' (v27).

Thomas replies, 'My Lord and my God!' (v28). This is the final affirmation to Christ in the Gospel and it reaches the highest level, declaring Jesus as God.

Jesus has the last word and it is for many '"Have you believed because you have seen me? Blessed are those who have not seen and yet have come to believe"' (v29).

The never-ending story (v30–31)

John ends by telling us he could have written more, 'But these are written so that you may come to believe that Jesus is the Messiah, the Son of God, and that through believing you may have life in his name' (v31). This is not just a story it is about the living Lord, who is the Messiah and the Son of God. Do you have a relationship with him? Do you know him? Or do you go back to the beginning and the words of John the Baptist: 'Among you stands one whom you do not know.'

Remember faith is not about knowing about Jesus, it is knowing Jesus the living Lord.

Ruminate *(in silence 5 minutes, shared 5 minutes)*

These are great events. Think of the wonder, the love and the deep emotions of Mary Magdalene. What must it have been like to touch her Lord once more? Note that Jesus is 'solid' and not a ghost. This was a miracle that had to be shared but how would Mary feel as the Lord sent her to the disciples? How simple her statement and how great her joy. Do you think the disciples would believe Mary immediately?

After Jesus appears to the disciples, Thomas appears. How can they convey what has happened? Note the demands of Thomas, he wants some proof! Imagine Thomas' reactions when being invited to touch Jesus. You may like to end with the words of Thomas and say to Jesus the living Lord, 'My Lord and my God.'

As a group

Give all the opportunity to say which of the disciples they would have like to have been at the resurrection and what difference the resurrection makes to them.

You may like to think further about the fact that by staying with those who had seen Jesus, Thomas was being prepared for the coming of Jesus.

React *(directed to God 5 minutes, shared with the group 10 minutes)*

In the silence give thanks for the resurrection and for the gift of eternal life. Give thanks for the risen appearances as recorded by St John. Rejoice in the presence of the risen Lord: he is here with you, talk to him. You may like to pray: Jesus may I know you in your risen power.

As a group

Give each one a chance to share what struck them most about the passage.

Choose some of these points to look at:

Think how often we still relegate Jesus to the past tense – that is to history – when he is the living Lord. He is alive and with us now. Let all have the opportunity to say what struck them about the passage and go on to discuss how we could each improve our relationship to the present Lord.

How often and how do you relate to the living Lord?

How often do we talk *about* him when we should be talking *with* him?

Together, think about how you could explain to someone that Jesus is not confined to history but is alive and with us now.

Does your church seek to show that Jesus is truly alive and with us?

Rest and rejoice *(in silence for 2 minutes, final prayers, music and blessing 5–8 minutes)*

There is no need for words. Simply rest in the presence and love of our living Lord. Enjoy being with him. If you need to stop your mind wandering bring it back with the words of Jesus, 'Abide in me as I abide in you' (John 15:4).

Final prayers and music
Choose someone to lead you in the following:

Risen Lord, you were known to Mary in the garden,
be known to us and set our hearts on fire with love for you.

Risen Lord, you came to your disciples, who met behind closed doors,
be known to us and set our hearts on fire with love for you.

Risen Lord, you walked with Cleopas and his companion on the road,
be known to us and set our hearts on fire with love for you.

Risen Lord, you showed yourself to doubting Thomas,
be known to us and set our hearts on fire with love for you.

Risen Lord, you appeared to the disciples by the Sea of Galilee,
be known to us and set our hearts on fire with love for you.

Holy and ever-living God we give you thanks and praise that Christ is risen. In dying he had conquered death and in rising again has opened for us the way to life eternal. Today we rejoice that you, Lord Christ, appeared to your disciples. We give thanks that you never leave us even when we doubt you or forget you.

We thank you for all your faithful people who, though they have not seen you, believe in you and reveal in their lives your risen power. Glory to you risen Christ with the Father and the Holy Spirit one God now and for ever. **Amen**

Risen Lord, we ask your blessing upon all your faithful people, all those who confess you as their Lord and their God. We remember all who meet in your name and talk of your power. We pray for study groups and theological colleges, for all who meditate on your word and who seek your presence. We bring before you all who are beset by doubt and disbelief and all who are reaching out to seek you, to touch you and to find you. May we all know you and the power of your resurrection. We ask this in your love, knowing that you died and rose again for us, Jesus Christ our living Lord. **Amen**

Hymn

Sing one of the following together:

Jesus Christ is risen today
Jesus stand among us
Alleluia! Give thanks to the risen Lord
Thine be the glory

The blessing

May you find in Christ the risen Lord
a sure ground for your faith,
a firm support for your hopes,
the assurance of love everlasting,
the promise of life eternal
and the blessing of God Almighty, the Father, the Son
and the Holy Spirit, be upon you and your loved ones,
now and evermore. **Amen**

Recollect

Take away with you a thought, a text or a resolution to use during the week. Always include in this a reminder of the presence and use it every day as often as possible.

Here are some suggestions:

'I want to know Christ and the power of his resurrection' (Philippians 3:10).

Each day rejoice in the presence of the risen Lord.

Throughout the day affirm his presence wherever you are and say: The Lord is here: his spirit is with us. Alleluia.